The Millionaires Hustle

Dylan Hasson

Copyright © 2021 Dylan Hasson

All rights reserved. No portion of this book may be reproduced in any form without permission from the publisher, except as permitted by U.S. copyright law.

For permissions contact: hello@dylanhassonofficial.com

www.dylanhassonofficial.com

Disclaimer.

The advice and strategies found within may not be suitable for every situation. This work is sold with the understanding that neither the author nor the publisher are held responsible for the results accrued from this book's advice. Individual results may vary, and testimonials are not claimed to represent typical results. All testimonials used in promotional material or any other applications are real participants, and may not reflect the typical purchaser's experience, and are not intended to represent or guarantee that anyone will achieve the same or similar results.

I have written this book based on my knowledge and experiences which have been unique to me. I am not a professional financial, marketing, business or life advisor and the content herein is not meant to replace professional advice. You are responsible for your own decisions and actions, and should you make a decision influenced by any information contained in this book or any of my media channels, you do so entirely at your own risk.

Hustle.

To have the courage, confidence, and motivation to go out and find the opportunities which will allow you to reach your goals.

Table of Contents

Introduction 6
Ask Yourself, "Why?" 9
Learn To Accept Failures! 13
Build A Brand! 28
Become Financially Smart! 33
Invest In Yourself! 36
View Money As A Tool, Not The Goal. 48
Respect Time. 50
Put Values Before Money. 52
A Few Last Words. 54
About The Author. 56

Introduction.

The word "Hustle" is generally viewed in a negative light. I didn't agree with most of the definitions that I found, so I made my own.

I believe that a positive or negative definition can be applied to "Hustle" depending on the individual person doing it.

This book is for people like me, with big aspirations yet feeling like you have no idea what you're doing half of the time. Highly experienced entrepreneurs may view the knowledge and views shared herein as lessons already learnt, but for the people starting out or already into their journey, I hope that what I have learnt over the last 14+ years will be of value. A belief that I have developed since starting my journey is that hustling your way to wealth has less to do with what you are doing and more to do with how you are doing it, having the right mindset and applying it to practically any hustle will significantly increase your chances of success.

The title of this book is attributed to you, the reader; if your goal is to become a millionaire and beyond, I am truly rooting for you. My journey continues, it's far from over, and I continue to learn and apply new knowledge. "The Millionaires Hustle" applies to each one of us on our own journey, making our own way, and I sincerely hope that this book leaves you feeling a little more knowledgeable, feeling a little less alone, and feeling a little more inspired!

Although it makes sense that when an unscrupulous person is out "hustling" to make a quick buck at the expense of other people, then a negative connotation is given. Fortunately, these types of people often don't get very far towards "making it big" and tend to stay on a low level because of their short-sightedness. Professions such as Real Estate Agents and Vehicle Sales are often unfairly seen negatively because of these unscrupulous people who were out to make a quick buck, yet they don't last long and work themselves out of their industries. I've met some of the most professional and admirable people who are Estate Agents, Vehicle Salespeople, etc., and many are highly successful in their hustle and have been doing it for many years – It's their mindset and reputation that allows them to be successful!

In order to make it big, you're going to have to think big and think long term. There's nothing wrong with starting out your hustle at a low level; earning your first million also involves earning your first hundred, your first thousand, and your first hundred thousand. No matter what level you start at, your hustle will grow with your own personal development, knowledge, skills, contacts, and reputation.

It doesn't matter what your hustle is – It can be anything! Flipping items for sale (buying and selling), selling vehicles or property, selling food, a product, or a service. You get to decide what definition of hustling applies to you, positive or negative. You get to decide if you want to become successful or stay at a low level. If you decide to stay at a low level, then there's really no reason to continue with this book. If you decide on success, this book is about my experience of "hustling" for the last 14+ years.

Although this book may not hold any "secret answer" to becoming wealthy and successful, I have written it based on the knowledge gained from what I have personally done and from what I have seen other successful people do. You get to decide what you do with the information from this book.

Ask Yourself, "Why?"

Often, I meet like-minded people. People who are on the same or similar journeys. Some of these people are at a similar place as myself, some are far ahead, and others are just starting out. It's always interesting to find out their "Why?" – Why did they start? What motivates them?

More often than not, the answer from the people just starting out is "Money". "I want to make more money!" Whereas the more experienced entrepreneurs often have completely different answers and goals. The more experienced people have in common, though, they've realized what their "Why?" is. They want to make a difference, make a change, want a better lifestyle or live their lives to their full potential.

Personally, I don't believe "to make more money" is a strong enough "Why?". I've been there! When I started out after school, I went out intending to make money, I created an advertising service, and I went out to sell it to businesses because I wanted to make money.

I only got so far…

Although I made a few sales, most businesses said "NO," and when you're starting out and constantly hear that "NO", your reason for just to make money, your "Why?" isn't strong enough to keep you motivated. Find a good reason as to why you're starting a business, why you're starting a hustle and offering your service. One of my biggest "why?'s" is because I hated having debt collection agencies harassing me. Yes, I'd have loved to own a bright red Ferrari, but more than that, I wanted to be debt-free! Another of my "why?'s" is because I wanted to provide a comfortable lifestyle for myself; I felt embarrassed to look at prices on the menu and then eat something cheaper instead of what I actually wanted to eat. I felt I wasn't living up to my potential, and that was a strong motivator for me, and it still is!

Once you have a powerful reason, your "Why?" will help you keep motivated through the difficult times. Most people want to earn more money, but do they? No – because it's not a strong enough motivator. Your "Why?" can be unique to you and your current situation, and once your situation changes, your "Why?" can change too.

You get to decide what your "Why?" is.

Over the years, I have tried many ventures; some worked well, others were OK, and many just failed dismally! My first reasonably profitable venture was in high school, and it was a concept I had learned from my dad – buying and selling (flipping items). At that time, my dad owned a used goods store, so I was able to learn the basics and apply them, and in my case, it was with trading cards. At that time, trading cards were a hot commodity with rare cards fetching high prices, so finding cards to buy and then resell became my first official "hustle".

Dylan Hasson

We didn't have the internet as we do today; back then, I had to buy the classifieds paper and browse through the adverts in search of cards and anything else that sounded like a bargain. The paper used to be issued on Thursday mornings, and my routine was after being dropped off at school, I would leave the school grounds and walk to the nearest convenience store to buy a copy of the paper and a coffee and walk back before school started. Our first period was an open period, so I spent it reading through the classifieds in search of trading cards, specifically sellers who had lost interest and were selling off their entire collections, etc. and making contact with the sellers. Throughout the school day, I would arrange suitable times to meet with the sellers, which would often be for the following Saturday, and then later in the afternoon break the news to my parents that I needed a lift to towns, sometimes an hour's drive away on the upcoming Saturday – This is something I will forever be grateful to my parents for as it allowed me to use and grow my entrepreneurial spirit. Saturday's meeting with sellers would come; I would assess the sellers' cards for sale and negotiate to purchase the lot. Once we got home, I would then organize the cards and get them ready for resale at school during the following week.

Although the money earned from this hustle was often small amounts, it was an invaluable lesson in business at that age which I consider to be the most important lesson I learned while in school, albeit a lesson that wasn't even learned from school. Because of this, I will always tell parents to encourage their children's entrepreneurial side if they show it. It's an invaluable skill to have in life, and it's a skill that can make them money, and it's a skill that can be used practically anywhere in the world!

Having an entrepreneurial mind will play a significant role in any hustle that you venture into, but I've also learned that having the mind for business is only one piece of the puzzle towards achieving success. Throughout the rest of this book, I will discuss the other skills or pieces of the puzzle that I've had to learn and implement.

Starting with the hardest…

Learn To Accept Failures!

Nobody wants to fail. Nobody starts a new hustle to fail, and sure as hell, nobody wants to fail repeatedly! – Too bad, it's probably going to happen, especially if you're new to the game! I've come to learn that failure plays a major role in the journey to success, it is a part of becoming successful, and for most of us, it's inevitable. The actual failure itself is not important, but the way in which we handle it – what we learn from it and how we grow from it.

At the time of writing this, I've probably failed more times than I've succeeded. I'm not embarrassed by that; instead, I'm proud – proud because I've failed more times than most people will ever even try, and that is a characteristic that has helped me succeed.

Failure forces us to think. It forces us to take a different approach, it forces us to adapt, and it allows us the opportunity to reinvent ourselves. I've never met a successful person who wouldn't acknowledge that they've never failed in some way or another along their journey. If you were to ask a successful person if they've experienced failure along the way, most would be open about it. Why? Because they also realize that failure was an essential part of becoming successful, their networks and friendship circles have experienced it and have also realized it is part of their journeys. Failure can build tenacity and motivate us to keep trying until we succeed, or it can create a fear that prevents us from trying at all. Having a fear of failure that prevents someone from ever trying only guarantees, they will not achieve their goals. While not fearing failure is a great advantage to any entrepreneur, they also need to be realistic to the fact that the possibility to fail always exists. Having the mindset of "This idea can't fail", "This business can't fail" is extremely dangerous; many of us have had this mindset, and more often than not, we get caught by surprise when things don't go according to plan and have no idea how to adapt. Experienced entrepreneurs are realistic about the possibility of failure, they understand that things don't go according to plan, they are able to identify areas where things could go wrong, and by doing so, they are prepared and are able to adapt when necessary.

A very relevant and personal example of a fear of failure is writing and releasing this book! "I'm not a writer; what if it's bad?", "Why would people listen to what I have to say?", "What if it doesn't sell?". - These are all questions that have all run through my mind while deciding to do this and to answer them, and I had to ask my "Why?".

"I'm not a writer; what if it's bad?".

Exactly, I'm not a writer, I'm an entrepreneur! I'll do it to the best of my ability and learn from it, but the important part is that I do it! Just as it's easy to say I'm not an experienced author, it's also an opportunity to learn and expand my own skillset. How do I become a better writer? By writing!

"Why would people listen to what I have to say?".

They don't have to. Nine hundred and ninety-nine people can completely not care about the book, but there's a chance that one in a thousand would be prepared to read it. If that one person can truly benefit from it and be motivated to start or try again, then I'll be happy to have made a positive impact in someone's life.

"What if it doesn't sell?".

Then it doesn't sell. Financial gain is not the only drive behind doing it, I want to do it! There's a time investment and a small financial investment to see it through. Am I prepared to take the risk? Yes, this book will become a part of my own hustle and journey; I'll be proud to see it through, and if it happens to become a financial success, then even better! Of course, I will apply all my business and marketing knowledge to this book with my own goals of making it a financial success, but fear of failure will not stop me from putting it out there!

Failure can only prevent you from becoming successful if you allow it, and being successful will not make you immune to failure. A person who has failed today could very well be successful in a year, just like a successful person today could fail in a year.

> *"Success is not final, failure is not fatal: it is the courage to continue that counts."*
> - Winston Churchill

Along with perseverance in overcoming the failures along your journey, having the correct knowledge is equally as important as never giving up. The correct knowledge can minimize our chances of failing, and the irony is that we gain knowledge by failing. It's one thing to have a great product or service, but if we don't know how to implement a strategy and sell it, the chances of failing are higher. Experienced entrepreneurs know that even having an average product or service can be a massive success by just having the right knowledge. A marketing strategy that works for one product may be completely ineffective for another, and this is where experience becomes invaluable.

I'm a massive fan of the "Dragon's Den" & "Shark Tank" series. It proves that you can have a room of highly successful people, each with their own knowledge, experience, and values to add to different people and products. The chances are good that each "Dragon" or "Shark" can make most products and ideas become commercially successful, but it doesn't mean they are automatically the right fit for the venture. They understand their strengths and networks and invest their time and money into the projects that can benefit the most from their own knowledge. The reward? The potential for massive financial gain in return for their knowledge and resources.

> *"Knowledge is of more value than gold."*
> \- Solomon

When it comes to mindset vs money, many entrepreneurs think that if they had the money behind them, their idea, product, etc., would automatically become successful. They could spend money to order more products, advertise everywhere, and customers would line up. In reality, this is rarely the case, and this way of thinking can be dangerous.

Money thrown at a product that doesn't sell due to poor design, not competitive or any number of reasons, or spent on the incorrect advertising channels without knowing the correct target market is money wasted. I would always advise entrepreneurs, especially new entrepreneurs, to develop their mindset and skillset before spending money aimlessly on their business or products. The "This idea can't fail" mindset could encourage an entrepreneur to spend their resources recklessly, and by the time they realize why their product is not selling, they may not have enough resources left to recover. By developing skills and mindset, by networking and speaking to experienced people and by testing and improving a product, it allows an entrepreneur the opportunity to make more informed decisions, take more calculated risks and ultimately give themselves a higher chance of succeeding.

Many entrepreneurs start off in the same way with a product or service, and with many entrepreneurs, the idea may be there, but a strategy to market is lacking or may be ineffective. Another common trait among many entrepreneurs which I have noticed is the "I'm just the creator, not the marketer" mentality, and they look at ways to outsource the marketing completely. In some cases, this may benefit the entrepreneur as it allows them more time to focus on product development and new ideas, but it can also be detrimental to their business if they don't understand the marketing strategy and its effectiveness. Many entrepreneurs also fall into the trap and temptation of "cheap" advertising, thinking they're saving costs but, in effect, could be throwing money away as the advertising they're paying for may be completely wrong and ineffective for their specific business needs. For this reason, an entrepreneur needs to understand exactly what their product or service achieves, who would benefit from their product or service, how their product will be seen, and how their product will be supplied to their customers. Understanding these fundamentals will give an entrepreneur an edge in their hustle; they will be able to recognize problems faster and adapt, they will be less likely to be done-in by suppliers, and they will have more overall control in their business and the direction in which they take it, even if they decide to outsource certain aspects.

Learn to develop the best possible product and keep on improving it.

For entrepreneurs who have created a new product, it's very easy for them to believe that their product is perfect and potentially overlook faults. Yes, believing in your product is necessary, but believing it is perfect and can't be improved upon is a dangerous way of thinking. When consulting with an entrepreneur who has developed a product, I always ask them what they believe is wrong with it or where they believe it can be improved upon. If they answer with anything along the lines of "nothing" or "nowhere" and refuse to be open to scrutiny, then I believe we would not be a good fit for each other and wish the person all the best on their journey. An entrepreneur who instead starts to think and look at ways to improve or may already have ideas of how they can improve the product is an entrepreneur who has a much higher chance of success. You're unlikely to be able to buy your own product to make it become commercially successful, so although entrepreneurs need to believe in their product, their market needs to believe in it too!

The market buying the product or service will determine if it becomes successful, and the reality is, the market has many options of products and services to choose from!

To have a competitive product and viable business idea, I believe an idea has to stand up to a few key elements;

What Problem Does It Solve?
Is It Visually Appealing?
Does It Offer Value?
Is The Demand Relevant?
Is It Scalable?

Although many more elements can be included, I look at these basic elements to decide whether or not an idea or product is viable to continue to invest more time and resources into.

What Problem Does It Solve?

There are many definitions of the word "Business". Essentially business is about solving problems. Entrepreneurs are people who are able to recognize problems, figure out ways of solving them, and, in theory, make a profit from doing so. The more efficiently an entrepreneur can solve a problem, the better the business.

"Necessity is the mother of invention."
— Plato

Many ideas and products are the results of an entrepreneur recognizing a need for them.

Is It Visually Appealing?

People tend to buy with their eyes, and the better something looks, the more we want it. It's human nature. A great product solves a problem and looks good while doing so. Even if you're offering a service instead of a product, a well-designed logo, use of colours, and thought-out branding can make your service look much more appealing than your competitors. Think of your product standing on a shelf with ten other brands. Does it stand out from the others? Does it draw attention and create interest? A well-designed and well-branded product can sell itself.

I'm someone who prefers healthier beverages to sugary ones, and with my recent move to the United Kingdom, I'm not familiar with many of the brands on offer – what do I do? I first look at the bottles that catch my attention the most, I quickly read the contents, and that's generally the product which I try first. If I don't like it, I'll try another brand next time on the same basis until I find one that I like, and I'll continue to purchase it. For all I know, there could be a much better product on the same shelf, but I wouldn't be inclined to try it unless someone recommends it to me.

Further on in this book, I discuss building a brand, and when creating a new product, especially in an already crowded market, putting in that little extra investment towards designing what your product looks like will go a long way towards creating a stronger brand.

Does It Offer Value?

> *"Price is what you pay. Value is what you get."*
> - Warren Buffet

The strongest products and services offer the best value for money to consumers, not the lowest price. The experience and perceived value a consumer gets from a product or service makes them purchase again and builds brand loyalty. Too many inexperienced entrepreneurs think that jumping into a market and offering a service and expecting their business to succeed simply because they're the "cheapest". Many highly successful businesses worldwide have been built based on offering the lowest prices, especially in the clothing and consumable goods industries. However, these businesses have a strong brand identity, offer their customers other conveniences, have immense buying power to purchase at the lowest possible rates, move their products in vast quantities and have exceptionally large financial backing – all elements that the average entrepreneur and small business doesn't have.

Yes, being the cheapest will attract customers – generally the cheap ones, and even then, if your customers don't believe they're receiving value, many will find it elsewhere even if the price is higher. Price doesn't build your customer base; value does.

Unfortunately, what tends to happen in industries with a low barrier to entry is that many wannabe "entrepreneurs" who don't understand business enter the industry and attempt to compete solely on price by undercutting everyone else, which leads many others to react by lowering their prices to stay competitive – this creates a vicious cycle and before long the industry is flooded by so-called businesspeople fighting for small scraps. This is what I've experienced in industries such as web development, social media marketing, estate agency, transport and logistics, etc, industries almost anyone can enter into. Although the industries themselves offer great potential and a rewarding career, the reality in them tends to be that most people are undercutting each other for scraps, and the only people making much money are those that understand how to charge their clients based on the value they provide instead of trying to be the cheapest. You may think that it would take years to reach this point, but that does not need to be the case. From day one, you could have the mindset of offering value to your clients and earn your worth – it is easier to start off as someone of value and build a reputation as such instead of starting off as someone cheap, building a reputation of being cheap and then trying to lose that reputation and building a new one of value.

To simplify it even further, would you prefer to spend your entire working day fighting for scraps or spend the same amount of time working with clients who are willing to pay for your value?

Still not convinced? Take a look at the worlds leading luxury brands such as Ferrari, Rolex, Hermes, etc. The cost to purchase their products is out of reach for most of the population, and yet they are world-famous, highly successful brands. Why? Because even at their cost, they offer their customers value, and their customers are happy to pay for it. These brands don't spend their time and resources making cheaper products to appeal to the mass market, and they focus on producing products that their established customers are happy to pay for and will always attract new customers who will pay for their value.

Anyone can lower their price, but not everyone can offer more value. Improve your skills and mindset, and you'll improve your value!

Is The Demand Relevant?

This question goes hand in hand with offering value. It's one thing to sell your product or service at a higher price because it offers more value, but is there a viable demand for it? Is there a big enough market willing to pay for it to build a sustainable brand and business from your product or service?

The demand for your product will also vary depending on where you are or plan to sell it in the world. A product or service that is in high demand in one area could also be unpopular in another. For this reason, an entrepreneur needs to understand who their target market is and if there is a demand for their product or service.

Your target market is never "everyone". "Everyone needs to eat" or "Everyone wears clothes" are dangerous and arrogant ways of thinking for entrepreneurs planning on selling food or clothing, etc. People have different dietary requirements, and we have different taste in shoes, so you're not going to sell your product to everyone. You'll sell your product to people whom it solves a problem. Your job as an entrepreneur is to research and work out if there is a big enough market that will purchase your product or service, which will vary from product to product.

Demand for a product can also fade over time; as the world goes through fads, the demand for certain items can spike drastically in a very short period, and the demand can fade just as fast. Remember the fidget spinner? Demand for the product soared when it became popular, and in what seemed like a relatively short period of time, the demand was steadily declining. Although the fidget spinner certainly seemed as if it was the most in-demand item during its peak, and I believe that many people and companies made substantial amounts of money, it did show that "the next big thing" runs its course and eventually gets replaced by "the next big thing".

Is It Scalable?

This process can take a small one-person or small team operation up to a recognisable national or global brand if that may be their goal. Most entrepreneurs won't expand their operations to this level for a variety of reasons, it's a challenging accomplishment to achieve without having the resources and network when starting, and it will often take decades to do. Each entrepreneur will have their own goals of how far they want to scale up their hustle, and each will have challenges unique to their circumstances. Growing from a one-person hustle up to a national brand can also seem like a daunting task for any entrepreneur, so when consulting with a client, I ask them:

"What can be done in the next 2-4 weeks to have a slightly bigger and more efficient operation?"

I find that many entrepreneurs stay a small operation by having the mindset of their product is great, so they're "waiting" for it to take off, they're "waiting" for the right person or company to see it, and almost overnight, they'll go from a small operation to a successful brand. The reality is they'll more than likely be waiting for a long time.

By asking what can be done in the next 2-4 weeks to have a slightly bigger and more efficient operation, it forces an entrepreneur to think of smaller and more realistic accomplishments.

Let's say you have a food product that you're making at home, and your goal is to have your product sold in stores throughout the country. Your product is brilliant – all your friends and family have told you so, so now all you need to do is produce 10 000 units per day, and you'll be set! The problems you find yourself with now are:

    a. You're unable to produce 10 000 units per day.
    b. You don't have the market to sell 10 000 units per day.

Unless you have the resources, an investor, or somebody in your network who believes in your product enough, realistically, your problems won't be solved any time soon.

So by thinking of what you can do in the next 2-4 weeks to have a slightly bigger and more efficient operation, you work with the resources that you have – you may not get your product in major stores around the country, but you could negotiate with local store owners and have your product available in 3 or 4 stores in your area. Another 2-4 weeks, and you can have your product in 3 or 4 more stores and perhaps produce your product for less in bulk. What does this achieve? Instead of spending a year "waiting" for the right person to see your product, you're now in 40 outlets. When that "right person" eventually does see your product, which looks like it's worth taking a risk on – the product that's being sold to friends and family or the product that's in 40 outlets?

That "right person" still hasn't seen your product after a year? No problem, you repeat your 2-4 weeks improvements for another year, and now you're in 100 outlets. Congratulations, your hustle has scaled up to a point where you have a brand that people are familiar with, and the demand is growing on its own, and you've realized that the "right person" has been you all along. If you build a brand, you will get approached eventually; the difference is that now with a strong brand behind you, you have much more negotiating power than you did two, four, or however many years ago.

> "You don't try to build a wall. You don't say, "I'm going to build the biggest, baddest, greatest wall that's ever been built." You don't start there...
> You say, "I'm gonna lay this brick as perfectly as a brick can be laid." You do that every single day, and soon you will have a wall."
>
> - Will Smith

As an entrepreneur, you get to decide where you want to scale your hustle up to, and if you intend to scale up, look at your scalability and break it down into smaller increments with realistic goals within your reach with your current resources. Even if it's not your intention to scale up, that's your choice, and you can still run a very profitable business as a one-person operation by improving all of the key elements mentioned above.

Build A Brand!

Whether you're going to take on the journey of entrepreneurship, starting a hustle and building a business, or work in a service-oriented career, you need to build a brand!

The next time you're passing through your city, take the time to notice the various businesses; which ones stand out? Which ones would you see in other cities? Or the next time you're walking through a retail outlet or convenience store, take the time to look at the various products on offer. Successful businesses and products have something in common – they have a brand! Even if your business doesn't sell products but offers a service, sell a branded service experience!

A sub-par product with a strong brand identity will outsell a brilliant product with a weak brand identity. Look at some of the most successful fast-food brands, the food may not be all that good or healthy, but the way the brand is promoted, the images used, the product presentation, the business systems in place, the convenience, the whole experience a customer gets is what sells the products. The brand which you build becomes the most valuable aspect of your business.

What is a brand?

A brand is something that is uniquely identifiable to you or your business. Your brand is your logo, your colour scheme, your brand tells a story to your customers and conveys emotion; your brand builds a relationship with your customers, your brand is an experience. Everything you do forms part of your brand - your brand is what convinces a customer to spend their money for the value it offers!

Great entrepreneurs build great brands while "wannabe" entrepreneurs do cheap imitations. There is no shortage of people without creativity trying to imitate every famous brand out there. Developing a brand is an area where an entrepreneur should spend time and money investing into. A strong brand is an asset; many world-famous brands earn vast sums of money just from licensing agreements by allowing other companies to use their branding! Companies will aggressively protect their brand because of the value it holds, so for entrepreneurs, building a brand while simultaneously building a business should be a non-negotiable priority.

People are brands, you are a brand! Look at any sports star or celebrity; they are brands! They can sell products based on the value their names hold to their fans and supporters. If these stars and celebrities do anything wrong that publicly tarnishes their name, their brand value suffers, and their sales can be affected. Just like famous people are brands, you as a person are a brand. As an entrepreneur, you are a brand and how you conduct yourself in your business and personal lives builds or damages your brand.

Why is it important to treat yourself as a brand?

Just like developing a product with its brand which resonates with its customers, you as a person do the same. Your customers may like your product or service, but they may be less likely to purchase from you if they don't trust you or dislike something about you. This can be tricky as we are humans; there will always be topics and issues that we will agree and disagree with one, but the reality is that people do form their opinions of us and those opinions play a role in their decisions to purchase from us. Social media is where people tend to form their opinions of other people based on the images and posts they see - when consulting with clients; I advise keeping their personal opinions out of their business matters as much as possible. People often post their own opinions whether outlandish, biased, factual, false, offensive, humorous, etc., on their social media feeds and are completely unaware of the harm it may cause to their brands. Roughly half of the world's population uses social media, so it's an incredibly powerful tool for marketing for entrepreneurs to tap into, and when using social media for business purposes, I advise my clients to remain neutral as much as possible; everyone has opinions, but keep opinions for friends and family. Understandably this is not always possible, and in many situations, it's good for a person and company to take a stance for a cause, but when a person makes an unnecessary post that is meant to be offensive towards a certain ethnicity, religion, sexual orientation, whether for the sake of humour or personal beliefs, it causes harm to their brand and reputation and dissuades people from supporting them.

What makes a successful brand?

Successful brands can identify their objectives; they understand the art of storytelling and providing an experience to their customers. Successful brands are capable of adapting to changes; they understand that what works today will likely not work in 5 years or ten years. Fashion, vehicle design, technology, architecture, health trends – the world is constantly changing, and brands that stand the test of time are the brands that adapt to the world around them and can provide what their customers want. Successful brands can "fit in" with current trends yet can "stand out" simultaneously. Entrepreneurs can, of course, also go the opposite route and create a brand that is in a niche of being old-school, rustic, retro, etc. but the same rules apply to create an effective brand, they need to be able to tell a story and create an experience to their customers.

One of my favourite brands of recent years is a relatively new brand called Zelos Watches. The entrepreneur behind the brand named Elshan Tang has, in my opinion, managed to perfectly create a brand within a very crowded market by applying all the rules of building a brand. His products are unique yet beautifully designed and offer exceptional value, and as a huge watch lover myself, the Zelos brand appeals to me. Elshan has also managed to create an extremely loyal community of watch lovers around the brand, and when new products are released, they sell out fast – proving that building such strong relationships and brand loyalty with customers creates a strong and relevant demand for the products. I would recommend for any entrepreneur to take a look at the Zelos brand as an amazing example of effective brand building.

Become Financially Smart!

Anyone can have all the knowledge in the world about how to market their product and how to develop their brand, but if they're not financially smart, they'll be working twice as hard to get half as far on their journey to success. Small, bad financial decisions will add up and hold anyone back just as effectively as small; good financial decisions will add up and allow financial freedom – it's that simple!

If someone asks me if I believe there's a secret to becoming wealthy, my answer is that I believe it's being financially disciplined. A person doesn't need to be an entrepreneur, own a business, or invent a product that's "the next big thing" to become wealthy; they can have a job earning a modest salary and become wealthy by being financially disciplined.

Although the concept is simple, becoming financially disciplined is not, this is where a person really must have a hard talk with themselves about what they want to achieve. The main reason that most people don't become wealthy is that they fall into the small traps of comforts and luxuries – "Small, bad financial decisions will add up to hold anyone back!"

Our online media and tv subscriptions, our shiny new phones, laptops and cars, our clothes on account, our ease of access to instant gratification, the comforts and luxuries we buy to feel good and impress other people – all these things purchased with salary earned income are small, bad financial decisions.

Sacrifice, sacrifice – reward!

People who can build wealth do so by not falling into these financial traps, or as a minimum, they purchase them with income earned from an asset as opposed to income earned from a salary. Many people will fall into these traps by thinking we earn 5000 per month, the new phone is only 150, so we convince ourselves that we can afford it. We then repeat this process with a vehicle, an online subscription, etc., and before long, we find ourselves paying for liabilities with salary income with very little or no money left. People who build wealth understand the importance of sacrificing these unnecessary "luxuries" and instant gratifications and instead look to purchase income-generating assets; they can use those assets to purchase liabilities.

As an entrepreneur building a business, sacrificing little luxuries will give you a much higher chance of success – your business, your brand, your hustle needs to be seen as an asset that requires investment. If you need some extra money for marketing, forget about the latest phone and invest that money into your asset! Forget about watching television; invest your time improving your service, researching more about your industry, reading, etc. One of the best rules I've learned to follow when purchasing a liability is to earn or save at a minimum, double the cost - if a phone costs 150 per month, invest into an asset or improve your hustle to earn a minimum of an extra 300 per month, by doing so, you will be growing your wealth and still earning more than you were before purchasing the liability. Even better, save until you have a minimum of double the amount and purchase cash! Not only does purchasing something like a vehicle cash save you on interest, but it also often allows you to negotiate a lower price, and often you will be able to sell the vehicle for more than what you paid for it – your vehicle could even be an investment if purchased this way!

Sacrifice, sacrifice, reward! By sacrificing instant gratification or the urge to purchase liabilities to impress other people, being financially smart, and investing in your assets, you will still be able to enjoy your luxuries. However, the true reward becomes that you get to enjoy those luxuries without them being to your financial detriment!

Invest In Yourself!

Probably the best investments a person can make, whether they're entrepreneurs or not, are investments in themselves. Continually investing in yourself in various aspects of your life will significantly affect your entrepreneurial journey.

Invest in yourself by learning from others:

There is a wealth of knowledge out there to gain from other people – people who have walked the journey you are on! A key trait that successful people have in common is that they understand the importance of learning. Different entrepreneurs, salespeople, coaches, etc., have faced different challenges along their journeys and have learned different ways of thinking and overcoming them. They also learn from others to better themselves and apply new strategies that may be more efficient; there is no "one size fits all" solution to becoming successful; it's about gaining and implementing the knowledge that works best for each person's situation.

Learn in ways that are convenient and best suit you; whether that be through books, audio, video, courses, seminars, coaching, etc., or a combination of them, there are many ways to learn and improve practically any skill you need.

The world's top entrepreneurs hold an incredible wealth of knowledge, and even they understand that they do not and will not know everything, they are open to learning because it's a means to staying relevant and on top of their game.

Invest in yourself by learning and improving your skills:

Learning new skills that go hand in hand with entrepreneurship will become invaluable! Some of the most valuable skills I've learned on my journey are:

- **Marketing:** Understanding the marketing process from idea to development to selling and refining your product will allow you to become an entrepreneur who can recognize problems and solutions faster. It gives you more control, and you'll make fewer mistakes on your journey – fewer mistakes mean you'll save money while promoting your product or service more effectively.

- **Web Development & E-commerce:** As someone who loves e-commerce, learning how to do web development and e-commerce has probably saved me the most money over the years. It allows me to set up new online ventures myself, then using knowledge of marketing, I'm able to test the viability of an idea with a minimum financial outlay.

- **Sales & Negotiation:** The success of your business comes down to how effectively you can sell your solution. The better the salesperson you are, the more effective you become. Whether you are selling a product or a service, you effectively sell yourself and negotiate the best possible deal. Being an effective salesperson requires you to adapt to the situation you're in, and that situation is always changing based on the people or companies you're negotiating with. Anyone in sales-oriented industries, such as real estate agents, vehicle salespeople, etc., will realize that they are always working with different types of people and personalities, and their success in their industries is largely dependant on how well they can work with and sell to their clients.

Having strong sales skills allow you to negotiate higher prices when selling and lower prices when purchasing, both impacting your overall wealth, so it's a high-value skill well worth investing in.

Sales industries such as real estate and vehicle sales are often seen negatively due to unscrupulous dishonest people who take advantage of their clients. Fortunately, their reputations generally catch up with them, and they eventually work themselves out of their industries. Unfortunately, there are always new people entering the market who are dishonest and willing to deceive their potential clients. The most successful salespeople I have met all have a common trait: their clients' best interest is their number one priority! They realize that by providing value to their clients, they build their brand and client loyalty, and as a result, they are high-earning individuals.

A huge benefit of learning these high-value skills is that they also allow you to earn an additional income by starting another side-hustle and charging other people and businesses for the service. Even if you're not interested in starting a business selling products, by investing in yourself and becoming very knowledgeable in any high-value skill, there will be people and companies willing to pay for your knowledge.

Invest in yourself mentally: Your mindset will play one of the biggest roles along your journey to success. Your mindset determines how you handle challenges, it determines how you handle failure, and it determines how you will keep yourself motivated. The high highs and the low lows of entrepreneurship are exceptionally mentally taxing – bluntly speaking, I believe only a small percentage of people are cut out to be an entrepreneur!

When things go well, you'll be praised, you'll be called "lucky", people will admire you for the things you have, and when things go badly, and you need to make difficult decisions, you may be thought of as the biggest asshole – very few people will understand what you go through and for the few that may, there's rarely anything they can do to ease the stress. Entrepreneurship is lonely with often little support and belief, so when things go well, and new people are attracted into your life, you'll naturally become sceptical and find it difficult to trust as you'll realize that when you make money, there will be no shortage of people willing to try to take it from you. From the outside, people often perceive entrepreneurship as glamourous, but within yourself, it can and will often be mentally and emotionally taxing and a rollercoaster of emotions, especially during the early days of a new venture. It's for all these reasons that I believe investing in yourself mentally is essential; we are human after all and can only handle so much.

Again, what may work for one person may not work for another, it's important to figure out what works for you as an individual – the following is what works for me:

- **Don't overdo it:** Although entrepreneurs can push their limits, overworking is a fast way to hit burnout. Building a successful business will take a combination of hard and smart work, and I've found that pacing myself is more effective than running at 110%. Many entrepreneurs, successful or not, tend to glamourize working upwards of 10, 12, 14 hours per day. If you're fully capable of doing this, then great, it's a strength that will help you along the way, but the reality is that not everyone can sustainably work like this. Work as hard as you possibly can, don't look for an excuse to be lazy, but if you're not capable of working 80 or 100+ hour weeks, it does not make you undeserving of becoming successful!

- **Set Your Goals:** Set small goals, set big goals, but set realistic goals! We're entrepreneurs; we hustle because we have goals that we want to achieve; otherwise, what would be the point? Our goals can be financial, lifestyle, health, making the world a better place, our goals can be anything, but we need to have them. Setting and achieving goals along our journeys keeps us succeeding and keeps us motivated. It's likely your goal is to be a millionaire, and while that is a great goal, why not break it down into smaller, more successive goals? More achievable short-term goals will help maintain your motivation and keep you eager to achieve the next target. At the beginning of this book, I said earning your first million also involves earning your first hundred, your first thousand, and your first hundred thousand - although earning a million might be the biggest goal, it shouldn't be the prioritized goal. Starting with almost no or limited resources and earning a million will feel like an almost impossible task but earning your first hundred will feel easily within reach – so aim for the hundred! Earning the second hundred will feel easier with the extra resources, and before long, you'll reach your first thousand. These small goals may seem insignificant, but they are effective milestones, and when you consistently feel like you're achieving, your motivation and energy levels stay up. Small, consistent successes add up, and as you gain more resources, earning a thousand or ten thousand or hundred thousand will start becoming as easy as earning that first hundred.

- **Don't entertain bullshit:** You've got enough on your plate; there's no need to take on unnecessary things that weigh you down more and waste your time without accomplishing anything. The world is full of drama and full of people who spend their days accomplishing nothing and gossiping about other people – let them be and walk away. If your friend's gossip, complain about everything, are not happy about your successes, and yet are doing nothing with their lives, bluntly speaking, you have the wrong friends! Entertaining bullshit also means keeping people in your life who do not support or believe in you, your true friends, network, some family, and the people you inspire will be the ones cheering for you; if not, they are only holding you back. Just as you shouldn't entertain bullshit from other people, you shouldn't entertain it from yourself either. "Bullshit" is the excuses we make why we can't do something. Can't afford to invest in yourself, but you have the latest phone? That's bullshit! Can't afford to start your hustle, but you can put new wheels on your bank-owned car? Yip, bullshit! We're all guilty of it in one way or another, and it's up to us to realize it and stop making excuses for why we can't and start finding reasons from why we can.

- **Be willing to pivot.** "Pivoting" in business means to change the direction or strategy of the business when the products or services are not meeting the market's demands. Many people may view pivoting as a "last-ditch" attempt to save a company, and while this may be true in many cases, I view pivoting as an opportunity to build a more efficient business. A good entrepreneur can adapt, and pivoting is a form of adapting to the feedback received from the market. A famous example of a pivot in business is Starbucks. The company did not start selling freshly brewed coffee but instead started in 1971 selling coffee makers and coffee beans. It wasn't until 12 years later, in 1983, after a visit to Italy where Howard Schultz decided to change direction, started selling a different version of their product, and turned Starbucks into the mega-brand it is today.

Dylan Hasson

"A pivot is a change in strategy without a change in vision."

- Eric Ries.

- **Invest in your health:** This one made a huge impact on me; I look better, I feel better, I think better! The phrase "feeling like a million bucks" became so applicable when I started taking my health seriously, and I experienced first-hand when feeling and emitting positive energy, I attract it back! A healthy mind allows you to make better decisions, and the better decisions you make, the more successful you become. Can't find enough time to exercise but have plenty of time to binge-watch series? I think you know what that's called…

- **Finding a mentor:** Finding a good mentor can be an incredibly valuable way to gain knowledge and boost your hustle. A good mentor can offer you guidance based on their own experiences, they can look at your business from a completely different angle to your friends and family, and they may also be able to open new doors and opportunities that you may not have otherwise had access to. A good mentor will also keep you accountable, but bear in mind that they will not be there to spoon-feed you, and should you be fortunate enough to find a mentor willing to spend some of their time guiding you, you will need to consistently show them that you are serious and worth their time investment.

- **People won't like you, be ok with it:** As you walk your journey, more and more people will just not like you. It will be a combination of friends, family, staff, competitors, random people, and for any number of reasons. It's normal, it's going to happen, and as an entrepreneur, you'll need to accept it.

> "If you want to make everyone happy,
> don't be a leader – sell ice cream."
> - Steve Jobs

See yourself as a leader: Even if you're working by yourself, you need to see yourself as a leader. All top entrepreneurs are leaders; they can guide teams and guide their clients and customers. If you are selling anything, a service, a new car, anything, your clients will look to you as a source of knowledge and often rely on that knowledge to decide. As a leader, you need to believe and be confident in yourself and your knowledge – you cannot expect your clients and customers to believe and have confidence in you if you do not have it in yourself.

"Don't overdo it. Don't entertain bullshit. Invest in your health. People won't like you...." – these are all qualities of being a leader. Being a leader means believing in yourself even when others don't; it means keeping yourself motivated. Equally important, being a leader also means recognising when you're wrong. Things go wrong all the time in business; leaders recognize when they need to slow down, take a step back, pivot and change direction and guide themselves, their teams, and their companies back towards the right direction.

A leader is also able to accept criticism. Criticism should not be taken personally; instead, it should be seen as an opportunity to learn and improve. Thank your customers and clients for their feedback, as few people will be honest enough to tell you when something is not up to standard. If criticism is made and directed at you out of spite and meant to hurt you, well, not everyone is going to like you, and that's OK. Look at the social media channels of almost any leader, celebrity, influencer, YouTuber, etc.; there will almost always be some sort of "comment warrior" in the comments who have something insulting to say towards them - the irony is the leader carries on and goes back to their life succeeding while the "comment warrior" often has nothing to go back to. Are you a leader making things happen or the comment warrior?

Believe that you are already wealthy and commit to that mindset: This is an effective "life-hack", you become rich in your mind long before you become rich in your bank account. This shifts your way of thinking from "I can't" to "How can I" – If your goal is to buy a Ferrari, you stop thinking, "I can't afford that Ferrari," and you start thinking, "My Ferrari is waiting for me". Committing to this mindset motivates you, and when you start feeling successful, it becomes a magnet for success. Thinking "I can't afford it" is demotivating, and it leaves no other outcome, if you believe you can't afford it then that remains your reality. Don't go around telling other people you are wealthy, tell it to yourself, wealthy people don't need to tell other people that they're wealthy.

"Poor" vs "Poor Mentality." There is nothing wrong with being poor if that happens to be your current situation. Many exceptionally wealthy people were born into poverty, it was their mindset and work ethics that made them rich and being poor was a part of their journey, they may have had to work harder, smarter and struggle for longer, but it was their journey and I'm certain many of them would say it made them become who they are. "Poor mentality" shifts the blame – saying "I don't have money because my parents didn't have money" is not taking responsibility and people who think like this don't move forward. Saying "I don't have money because I've made poor financial choices, but I'm determined to change that" is already taking responsibility.

Struggling financially yet having a "wealthy mentality" will get you infinitely further than struggling and having a "poor mentality".

Be proud of and appreciate what you already have: If you don't appreciate what you already have, why do you think you deserve more? It's OK to want more, it's OK to want a better car and a better house, but there are millions of people who wish for and would appreciate the things you have! Learn to truly appreciate what you have now so that you'll appreciate your future successes. This mentality will also help you stay positive and motivated, if you keep focusing on the things you don't have it will become demotivating.

Be genuinely happy for other peoples' successes: "Poor mentality" tends to make someone dislike a wealthy person just because they're wealthy. They'll convince themselves that a "rich person" must have taken advantage of other people to become rich, when most of the time it can just be attributed to jealousy. As an entrepreneur, you would know that success does not come easy, so when other people achieve success, big or small, be happy! If your friend has just achieved buying their dream car, be genuinely happy for them! Remember, your successful friend already knows not to entertain bullshit, so if you are not someone who can cheer for others, you'll be left behind faster than you realize.

Find your balance: Success requires sacrifice, there is no getting around that, but there is no point in sacrificing things that money cannot buy. Spending your life only focussed on chasing money is going to lead to an unfulfilled life, this is something I believe many people realize too late. It's not glamourous to sacrifice your health for money, even if you do become rich, you'll more than likely spend your money trying to get your health back. It's not glamorous to burn yourself out trying to become successful in two ye,ars whereas working within a balance may take you five years – the time will pass regardless. The sacrifices we make should be materialistic and instant gratification, and of course, we need to sacrifice time and work hard, but to sustain that hard work, we need balance.

It may sound like a cliché, but I believe it to be true – we become what we allow ourselves to absorb. If we spend our time absorbing negativity and doubt from others, focusing on what is wrong in our lives instead of what is right, we become that negativity. It becomes easy to see what is negative when we and our peers are looking for what is negative, just the same as it becomes easy to see opportunities when we and our peers are looking for opportunities!

View Money As A Tool, Not The Goal.

It's OK to love money and it's OK to want more money - I love money and I want more money! But to me, money is not the goal, it's a tool to build more wealth. Sure, we'd all love to have tens or hundreds of millions in the bank, but for most wealthy people, it's not about the money, it's about the experiences and lifestyle that the money can afford them. Money is a tool to build a portfolio of assets that continuously earn more money to sustain the lifestyle and experiences.

If money was the goal, by that logic every person who wins a fortune in a lottery would be able to maintain the lifestyle their newly acquired fortune allows them – yet a quick online search reveals that as high as 70 percent of lottery winners go broke. There will always be various reasons for this, but for the majority it will be due to a lack of financial education, they do not acquire assets and instead acquire more liabilities. I believe that all the lessons we learn along our journey make us financially intelligent and it's those lessons that equip us to handle wealth correctly and create more wealth.

"If I had more money, I could fix my problems..." This is one of the most frustrating examples of "poor mentality" thinking which I regularly come across. So many people simply believe that if they had enough money, they would sort their lives out.

How? Would you pay off debts and magically know to stop making bad financial decisions? Be honest with yourself, would more money fix your problems, or would better decisions fix them? More money without knowledge can temporarily fix problems just as easily as it can create more problems – If you're making small poor financial decisions now all that having more money will do is allow you to make bigger poor financial decisions. "More money" is not the solution, you are the solution, your mindset is the solution! Money is merely a tool, and your decisions determine if that tool helps build a financially successful life or a financially stressful life.

Respect Time.

Respect your own time and respect the time of others. I believe that the two most important assets any person has, whether they're an entrepreneur or not, is their mindset and their time. You can lose money and earn it back, but you can never get back lost time!

Wealthy people can leverage their money to gain more time for themselves, their families, and doing things they love, whereas most people will spend their lives exchanging their time for money.

Many years ago, my dad explained to me that the greatest gift a person can give, is their time. With this belief and respect for time, I try to use my own time efficiently and my clients' time efficiently, so that I have more time for experiences that I enjoy. I've come to despise wasting my time, many people would say I'm impatient, but I am extremely patient when it's necessary, I just have no tolerance for my time being wasted – whether by me or other people. Respecting other people's time makes doing business much more efficient and it becomes a trait that people appreciate when doing business with you. Ironically, the people who will tend to waste the most of your time are usually the people who can least afford it. Another way to look at it is the more a person earns, the more valuable their time becomes, so whether you're earning a high income yourself or doing business with someone who is earning a high income, you are effectively costing yourself and them money by babbling on! I will use this very book as an example, it may be criticized for being a short book compared to many others in the same genre, but I value your time as my reader, so I would prefer if you spent an hour reading and hopefully finding value in it instead of 5 hours reading the same points in different words.

Put Values Before Money.

One of my favourite and most important lessons I've learnt was from two separate job interviews.

In 2014 and 2017 I had two interviews with two real estate principal status agents (business owners). During my interview in 2014 with "Principal A", after being asked why I wanted to become a real estate agent, I had explained my various reasons and after a long discussion he told me "You forgot to mention the most important reason which is to make lots of money." I had figured that "making lots of money" would have been a direct result of applying my reasons I had given him, but it was clear we had different opinions and needless to say, I didn't join his company.

During my interview in 2017 with "Principal B" it was immediately clear the vision was different. The values displayed on the wall of the company read "People First. Doing The Right Thing. Being Courageous. Fun & Laughter." The interview was with Mr. Steve Caradoc-Davies, who at the time was the business owner of South Africa's #1 Harcourts Agency and has since gone on to become the CEO of Harcourts International. During the interview it was clear that Steve's priority was whether or not the brand and I were a good fit for each other and if I would fit in with the rest of the team, not scrutinizing if I was there to "make lots of money".

I was fortunate enough to have been able to join the company, learning directly from some of the most knowledgeable people in the industry. Steve and many of my colleagues became mentors, and my time with the company has made a significant impact on my entrepreneurial career as the knowledge I gained there has been invaluable.

Putting strong values before money will at times cost you money, you may miss out on sales, but your customers and clients will value you for it and the sales you may lose will be made up for. Whether you put values before money or money before values, your reputation will catch up to you and it's that reputation that will often determine if you will have a long and successful career or work yourself out of the industry.

When considering a new opportunity in a sales career or if you are currently working in one, be mindful of the "Leadership" team and their ethics. They will influence the way you do business and if they pressure you to make sales "at all costs" keep in mind that those "costs" are borne by your clients and your reputation.

A Few Last Words.

Although I've tried to keep quotes to a minimum unless I felt they were relevant and applicable to the subject, the following is from a song by Hopsin, one of my favourite musicians:

"Change is one of the most difficult things that we face
But change is inevitable
One reason we don't like change
Is we get comfortable where we are
We get used to our friends, our job, the place we live
And even if it's not perfect we accept it, because it's familiar
And what happens is, because we're not willing to change
We get stuck in what God used to do
Instead of moving forward into what God is about to do
Just because God's blessed you where you are
Doesn't mean you can just sit back and settle there
You have to stay open to what God is doing now
What worked five years ago may not work today
If you're going to be successful
You have to be willing to change
Every blessing is not supposed to be permanent
Every provision is not supposed to last forever
We should constantly evaluate our friendships
Who's speaking into your life?
Who are you depending on?
Make sure they're not dragging you down
Limiting you from blossoming
Everybody is not supposed to be in our life forever

Dylan Hasson

*If you don't get rid of the wrong friends
You will never meet the right friends."*
- Marcus Hopson

I believe these words above are one of the best pieces of advice that can be given to anyone as they can be applied to entrepreneurship and our lives in general and they have made an impact on my outlook and way of thinking.

As entrepreneurs, we are go-getters, we become efficient and we like to get things done ASAP – while these are all important traits to have, I believe it is just as important to remind ourselves that success is not a race! We are not competing against anyone to be better or richer than them, although it is good to be competitive where it matters, the journey we each walk towards our idea of success is our own journey. Some will reach success fast; some will reach it over many years and sadly many others will never reach it.

Be disciplined and strict on yourself, remind yourself of your "why's" when you need to, but at the same time also be forgiving on yourself – it's normal to feel frustrated or like you're failing when things don't work out as expected, but you've made it this far, so stand back up, dust yourself off, learn and hustle on!

I'd like to thank you for your time and reading this book – I truly hope that you have found value in your investment, and I wish you the success you seek on your journey.

Dylan Hasson

About The Author.

Dylan grew up in the Helderberg region, an area just outside of Cape Town, South Africa. His first official business venture at the age of 21 was an online directory dedicated to promoting businesses, the platform was eventually sold.

Over the span of his entrepreneurial career, he has ventured into many businesses and investments, including transport, recycling and property development with his father, real estate consulting, e-commerce, and becoming a marketing consultant and working with large national brands and franchise owners.

www.ingramcontent.com/pod-product-compliance
Lightning Source LLC
Chambersburg PA
CBHW080952220526
45465CB00008BA/3250